Brighten the Corner

and 45 other women's devotions

by
Donna Clark Goodrich

STANDARD PUBLISHING
Cincinnati, Ohio   2270

Dedicated
To Gary, who has
"brightened every corner"
of my life

*

Library of Congress Catalog No. 72-82086

© 1972
The STANDARD PUBLISHING Company
Cincinnati, Ohio
Printed in U.S.A.

Contents

Brighten the Corner

"Ye are the light of the world" (Matthew 5:14).

Many years ago a lady by the name of Mrs. Ina Ogdon gave up a brilliant professional career to care for her invalid father. It was difficult for her, one used to appearing before thousands, to minister in private life to just one person. However, instead of pining away in self-pity because she could not follow her chosen career as a concert singer, she penned the words:

Do not wait until some deed of greatness you
    may do,
  Do not wait to shed your light afar,
To the many duties ever near you now be true,
  Brighten the corner where you are.

One young woman felt definitely called to the mission field but her health did not permit her to go. She felt very frustrated until one day she came to the conclusion that she could help and encourage the young people she knew. If one of them, through her encouragement, was led to go to the mission field, she could in a sense feel that her call was fulfilled. Since that time several of her friends have gone, and now she writes to them, assuring them of her prayers and support.

We may think our light is small, but even one candle will light up a dark room. Perhaps we may be teaching a Sunday-school class instead of serving as a missionary in Africa, or playing the piano for the Junior Department instead of being a concert pianist, but each job done for Jesus is important.

Our work as housewives and mothers can take on a whole new perspective if we think of it as working for eternity. We can be ready with that word of sympathy for the skinned knee; the words of counsel for that first case of "puppy love"; words of spiritual wisdom as our children seek for God's will in their career and marriage plans. And sometimes we can "brighten the corner" just by being silent—by listening when they want to talk.

We can brighten not only our families, but whole neighborhoods by being that one person who won't give in to petty gossip; who will be there when someone needs to talk; who will have the coffeepot ready for someone with a burdened heart.

Perhaps you are not now where you once dreamed of being, but if your life is completely consecrated to Christ, you can "brighten the corner where you are."

Heavenly Father, consecrate my life that it may be used to brighten the world about me. In the name of Jesus, the true light, amen.

Here's the Mailman

"Thy word have I hid in mine heart, that I might not sin against thee" (Psalm 119:11).

You are expecting a very important letter. Perhaps it is from a son in the service, or a daughter away at college, Mom and Dad, your husband who is away on business, or a very special friend. You rush to the door as soon as you see the mailman coming up the steps, or maybe you have been waiting for him by the mailbox. He hands you a pile of letters and you hurriedly go through them. There it is!

You open your special letter eagerly and begin reading, starting with the salutation and finishing with the closing word. Later, you read it again, slower this time, to catch anything you might have missed the first time. Some parts you read over and over until you know them from memory.

How welcome is a letter from a loved one, and especially so when it contains good news! You know, your best Friend has written you a letter and it contains the good news that no matter what you have done, He still loves you and wants to forgive you.

The letter we speak of is the Bible. God is the author. You need to read the Bible just as you would a long-awaited letter. You wouldn't think of starting to read in the middle of a letter. It wouldn't make sense to you. So it is with the Bible. Systematic reading is very important so that we understand what the Author is trying to tell us. Later, go back and read the parts that are particularly appropriate to your situation. Memorize passages that are especially meaningful to you.

Develop a plan for reading the Bible through once a year. You say you don't have time to do that? How much time do you spend watching TV, talking on the phone, reading the newspaper, or working a crossword puzzle? The song says, "Take time to be holy," not find a few odd moments. We seem to take the time to do the things we want to do.

Have you ever received a letter then eagerly called someone to tell him what was in it? Why not try this with the Bible? Share it with a friend. And remember, put what you read into action for you may be the only Bible your friends read.

Many people read the Bible while on their knees. Why not try this today? Ask God to help you understand His Word, and then to put it into practice.

Heavenly Father, thank You for Your Word. May we ever use it in our lives. In the name of Jesus, amen.

From Mountaintop to Valley

"Master, it is good for us to be here: and let us make three tabernacles; one for thee, and one for Moses, and one for Elias" (Mark 9:5).

What a sight! How could they ever forget it? Christ had taken Peter, James, and John up into a high mountain. They were meditating and enjoying the cool air when suddenly Christ's "raiment became shining, exceeding white as snow." Elijah and Moses appeared and talked with Jesus. Peter, James, and John were frightened and astonished.

Then Peter asked if they could stay there—no problems, no trials, just the presence of God. But Christ made no answer, except to tell them not to tell any man what they had seen.

The disciples must have been somewhat disappointed as Christ led them down the mountainside. They were saddened because they could not stay in that heavenly place, and probably a bit dejected because they could not tell anyone about it.

We wonder why Christ did not let them stay on the mountain. We too have had these times when we were praying and felt far from the problems of life. How we wished we could go on like that forever. But we had to "come down from the mountain." Why?

If we're always on the mountaintop, we lose the vision of the people below. When Christ meets with us in a special way, it's hard to forget the emotion and go into motion among those who need our help. On the mountaintop, we lose the joy that comes from helping others. Our salvation develops into a mere self-centered religion. We're always expecting to receive, without wanting to give out.

Adam Clark makes the comment that this transfiguration took place in the night. This is an interesting thought to ponder—often our greatest mountaintop experiences come when everything seems the darkest. The night was not dark for Peter, James, and John, however, because they were walking with Christ. If we walk with Christ in the light, He will walk with us in the darkness.

Let us, after our mountaintop experiences, come down and take the vision of Christ to the "multitudes, multitudes in the valley of decision" (Joel 3:14) that they too may receive strength to climb the mountain and meet Christ face to face.

Heavenly Father, give us mountaintop courage and inspiration that we may be able to work in the valleys. In the name of Christ, amen.

What Is Your Life?

"What is your life? It is even a vapour, that appeareth for a little time, and then vanisheth away" (James 4:14).

We've heard teen-agers ask, "Why am I here?" Surely this thought has echoed in the minds of adults as well. Mothers may wonder, "Is this all there is to life—washing diapers, doing dishes, blowing noses, cleaning up messes, and washing sticky hands?"

The husbands may think, "Can we ever get ahead? Seems like my paycheck just won't cover all the necessities, say nothing of extras now and then." And so we ask ourselves, "Is it worth it?"

Paul must have wondered the same thing, but it seems as though he found the answer as he wrote, "None of us liveth to himself, and no man dieth to himself" (Romans 14:7).

A mother found herself especially depressed one day as she thought about how fast her life seemed to be going by, and how little she was accomplishing. As she knelt in prayer, God seemed to show her how important was the example she had set for her children. The moral standards she had taught them, even when her life was over, would still be living on in whatever her children accomplished during their lifetimes.

Our discouragement often comes because we cannot see the results of our labors. Paul says in 2 Corinthians 4:18, "We look not at the things which are seen, but at the things which are not seen: for the things which are seen are temporal; but the things which are not seen are eternal."

What is life? Are we here merely to find happiness for ourselves? No, for it is through sharing the joys we have found with others less fortunate that we find our purpose in life. Loving the Creator who made us, loving our neighbor as ourselves, loving the unlovable, we find our place in life.

> Lives of great men oft remind us
> We can make our lives sublime,
> And departing, leave behind us,
> Footprints in the sands of time.
> —*Longfellow*
> "A Psalm of Life"

Lord of heaven and earth, help us to see those about us who are waiting for the help we can give. May we ever be willing to use our lives for Your cause. In the name of Christ, amen.

Just Lovin'

"We love him, because he first loved us" (1 John 4:19).

While walking past a church building one day, a lady saw a little girl come out by herself. It was not Sunday so the lady asked, "Was there a church service today?"

"No," the child answered, "I was just praying."

The lady thought the girl might have some problem so she asked, "What were you praying for, dear?"

The girl replied, "Nothing. I was just lovin' Jesus."

How long has it been since you knelt in prayer just to "love Jesus"? So often our prayers are selfish. We pray because we have a burden. We pray because it is the right thing to do. We pray because we have gotten into the habit. But do we kneel just to say, "Lord, I love you"?

A mother was busy cleaning one day when she heard her small son burst through the door and call, "Mommy, Mommy, where are you?"

"In here, dear," was the instant reply. "What's wrong?"

"Nothing," the child answered, as he hugged his mother, "I just wanted to love you," and he ran outside to play.

Perhaps that is what Christ meant when He told us we should become as little children—impulsive, warm, loving. Zacchaeus eagerly offered to give up half of his wealth to the poor in order to please Jesus! Mary showed her love by pouring expensive ointment on Christ's feet and wiping it with her hair. Joseph of Arimathaea loved Jesus so much that he buried Jesus' body in his own tomb.

As we love God more, He will give us more love for others. We will become a channel through which His love can flow out to a lost and dying world.

Henry Drummond in his book, *The Greatest Thing in the World* makes this observation: "How better can we love? What makes a man a good artist, a good sculptor; a woman a good stenographer? Practice! What makes a good man? Practice. Nothing else."

How can we better love God? Practice! Sometime today tell God, "I love you."

Kind heavenly Father, may we ever show our love for You by loving others. In Jesus' name, amen.

Follow the Leader

"I am the Lord thy God which . . . leadeth thee by the way that thou shouldst go" (Isaiah 48:17).

One beautiful Saturday afternoon in Kansas City, a leader took her junior girls for a hike. At the end of the long two hours, they discussed some of the spiritual lessons they had learned that day.

First, they had to follow the leader. Some of them had never been on that trail before, but one girl had, and she went ahead. And the girls did not try to go ahead of her.

So, in our spiritual lives—the way is new to some of us, but we have a Leader. And as foolish as it would have been for the juniors to go in front of their hike leader, so it is foolish for us to try and go ahead of God, and expect Him to follow us.

Lead, kindly Light, amid th' encircling gloom,
    Lead Thou me on!
The night is dark, and I am far from home;
    Lead Thou me on!
  Keep Thou my feet; I do not ask to see
  The distant scene; one step enough for me.
             J. H. Newman

Second, the girls found that there were times of waiting! Often the guide would go ahead and see what was in the path before them. Perhaps there were briars or brambles, unknown to them. Occasionally, she would just give them a chance to rest.

Christ, in going ahead of us, often tells us to wait. There may be many reasons. He knows when we are weary. Perhaps that is why He allows a time of illness. "They that wait upon the Lord shall renew their strength" (Isaiah 40:31). When we are flat on our backs, the only way we can look is up.

It has been said that not only does the Lord order the steps of a good man, but also his stops. "In everything give thanks." We should thank God for the rest stops along the way. Even a beautiful piece of music has a rest now and then.

The third lesson the girls learned was that after their guide went ahead to survey the path, she returned to walk with them. Christ walked our road before us. In the wilderness, He walked the path of temptation. When His friend Lazarus died, He walked the path of sorrow. In the garden of Gethsemane, He knew temptation—and victory. He knew hunger, and weariness, and loneliness. And He will walk our road with us.

We must follow our Guide; we must stop when He bids us stop; and we have the assurance that He will "be with us always, even unto the end of the world." Let us start walking today.

Eternal Father, we thank You for our guide, Jesus Christ. Help us to follow where He leads. In His name, amen.

These Little Ones

"And whosoever shall offend one of these little ones that believe in me, it is better for him that a millstone were hanged about his neck, and he were cast into the sea" (Mark 9:42).

It was during the time that a series of earthquakes was violently shaking the coastal cities of California. Parents with a particularly active boy were worried because they could not keep him away from the shattered buildings, so they put him on a train and sent him to an uncle's home in Arizona. Two weeks later they received a telegram from the uncle, "Returning Randy on 5:45 train. Send earthquake."

Even the quietest children have days when it seems all they do is think of mischief. While we clean up one mess they made, they are into something else. Even after they pass the "spilling" stage, they can still manage to disrupt the household. But, oh, the potential in these children! How a mother should pray that she will have the grace and patience to teach these little ones about Christ and to lead them to Him.

An eight-year-old boy came running into the house, shouting as usual. "Mother, I need your help. We have to write an auto . . . auto, anyway the story of our life for school."

"Autobiography?" his mother supplied the missing word.

"Yeah, that's it," he replied. "Can you help me?" The two sat down and went through the usual facts: where he was born, places he had lived, members of his family. Then they got to the question of what he wanted to be when he grew up. This puzzled the boy.

"I'm not sure if I want to be a preacher or a baseball player," he admitted. The mother told him that whatever he decided, he must pray about it first and let God lead him. He said he would like to be a preacher but didn't think he could. Again his mother reminded him that with God's help, he could do anything. The boy's face brightened and he agreed, "Yeah, cause God knows more big words in the Bible than I do."

And the mother prayed as she went through that day, "Lord, help me not to plan my children's lives, even though there may be something I want them to be. As I dedicated them to Thee when they were born, let me keep that consecration complete. Lord, have Thy will with my children."

May that ever be our prayer.

More Like the Master

"We would see Jesus" (John 12:21).

More like the Master I would ever be,
More of His meekness, more humility;
More zeal to labor, more courage to be true,
More consecration for work He bids me do.
—*Charles H. Gabriel*

A man had a Chinese plate he valued very highly. One day the plate fell and cracked down the middle. The man ordered six more plates made and to insure the exact pattern, he sent his broken plate as a copy. When he received the package from China six months later, he was astonished to find the Chinese craftsmen had so faithfully followed his copy that each new plate had a crack right down the middle.

Whom are we copying? If we follow even the best of men, we are bound to imitate some of their imperfections. Why pattern our lives after an imperfect model?

Since we are made in the image of God, does it not seem logical that we should try to be like Him, and strive for His attributes? If we must imitate someone, let it be Jesus. Then we will show forth the fruits of the Spirit, "Love, joy, peace, longsuffering, gentleness, goodness, faith, meekness, temperance" (Galatians 5:22, 23).

The story is told about a remote little village in the hills of New England. Above the valley, a face was etched on the stone of the mountainside by wind and rain. It was a face full of calm repose, deep contentment, and spiritual uplift. It was believed that someday there would be someone in that valley whose face would resemble that of the great stone face. And Ernest, who was a little boy when the story opened, watched as the men who had gone out from that valley to become warriors, thinkers, and statesmen returned, and people would compare them to the stone face.

Daily Ernest worked and daily he looked toward the mountain. And then, when he was old and silver-gray, people began to see in Ernest, the humble workman and quiet citizen, the same qualities that were possessed by the great stone face. He had looked to the face for so long that he had become one with it.

Whose face are we looking at today? The more we see Jesus, the more of Him others will see in us.

Heavenly Father, may we ever look to Jesus as our perfect model. Help us to become more like the Master each day of our lives. In His name, amen.

A Firm Foundation

"He is like a man which built an house, and digged deep, and laid the foundation on a rock: and when the flood arose, the stream beat vehemently upon that house, and could not shake it: for it was founded upon a rock" (Luke 6:48).

It was a tremendous story. It was on television and in the largest newspapers. A partially constructed building had collapsed, killing ten men. What had happened? A cheap material had been used in the foundation and it could not stand the strain.

It was a small story. No newspapers carried it. It was not on television. A home had collapsed, killing the marriage of two adults and injuring several children. What had happened? There was a weak foundation that could not stand the strain.

What had weakened the foundation of this marriage? Perhaps it was not strong enough in the beginning. Maybe there was only physical attraction that sometimes quickly fades away. Perhaps the couple's friends were all getting married and they wanted to be "one of the crowd."

Then again, the foundation could have been laid with the best of materials but the building itself was not constructed properly: too much nagging; lack of privacy; forgetting to compliment; failure to budget; interference from well-meaning relatives; no time for anything except "getting ahead"; and, most important, too busy for church, prayer, or Bible reading. And the walls began to crumble. "If a house be divided against itself, that house cannot stand" (Mark 3:25).

A little boy, standing between his mother and father at church during prayer, linked one arm with that of his mother and the other through his father's. What a picture of security he made! And it is so with a marriage—God in the middle, one arm linked with the husband, the other with the wife. The eternal triangle!

Each for the other, and both for the Lord,
Living in accordance with His Holy Word;
Striving, and praying, and making their home
A refuge where each is safe from the storm.

Eternal God, may You ever be the center of our hearts, our homes, and our nation. In the name of Christ, amen.

Waiting for the Frosting

"Eye hath not seen, nor ear heard, neither have entered into the heart of man, the things which God hath prepared for them that love him" (1 Corinthians 2:9).

A certain woman was known throughout the neighborhood for her mouth-watering cakes with luscious chocolate frosting. She discovered, however, that the children were eating the frosting first and sometimes leaving the rest, so she began cutting off the frosting and giving it to the children after they ate the bottom half of the cake.

Leaving the frosting till last! Isn't that a somewhat basic rule of life? When we get the mail, we often hurry through the "junk" mail, the statements, the advertising, before settling down to read a long-awaited letter from a faraway friend or relative.

Many housewives will do the hard pieces of ironing first so they can get to the handkerchiefs and pillow cases that go so fast. Or we will rush through household tasks to sit down and enjoy a favorite television program, or a book that has been sitting on the shelf. We leave the best till last!

Perhaps that is what God is doing. John 14 tells us that Jesus has gone away to prepare a place for us, but we have to do some living first. We must put up with a few illnesses, some grief, and some trials, but He is leaving the best until last! In His Word God has given us an idea of what heaven will be like, but we will never know all the wonders until we get there.

An old missionary, returning from a long term of duty, was cheered as he saw the crowds of people waiting on the shore. He had not been forgotten after all. But then his countenance fell as he realized the people were there to greet a well-known film star. "Lord," he wept, "I've given my life for Thee. Is there no one to meet me now that I'm coming home?"

"Son," the Lord seemed to say, "Remember, you're not home yet."

It may seem as though our trials and discouragements are many but we must be patient and remember that "we're not home yet," and someday will come the "frosting."

Gracious Father, give us strength to live our lives for You each day. We thank You for the promise of a better place when this life is over. In our Saviour's name, amen.

Sermon at the Sink

"For ye make clean the outside of the cup and of the platter" (Matthew 23:25).

Two girls were helping their mother clean the kitchen one day. As they worked, the mother took advantage of the time being spent with her daughters to teach them some lessons of life.

As she cleaned the canisters, normally a very boring and dull task, the Holy Spirit showed her some valuable insight which she could share with the two young girls.

When she finished washing the outside of the canister, the mother showed the girls, that though the outside was clean, the inside of the tea canister was stained where some tea bags had broken open. She told her girls that there are many people who have cleaned up the outside of their lives. Their appearance is very pleasing, and they often attract attention as they appear in public. But they have failed to do anything about the inside. Their hearts are stained and soiled by sin.

Then she explained to them that in order to keep

the contents clean, the inside of the canister also has to be kept clean. And to have clean words and actions, the heart has to be cleaned out by Jesus Christ, and we must keep it clean.

After the canisters were sparkling, inside and out, the mother noticed that where they had been standing in the corner, a dull spot remained which hadn't been cleaned in a long time. Also the wall behind the canisters was in need of a scrubbing, and this the three of them did before replacing the canisters.

Environment! How important it is to keep the children's surroundings free from tension and strife, to give them the right friends and the proper activities. The mother searched out her own heart as she thought of times when she was "too busy" to read the Bible to the girls or share with them some wonder of nature.

Perhaps we should all have a clean-up day—first making sure our hearts are completely clean, that there is nothing in them that will stain or soil. Then we can work at making the outside attractive so that we may be more effective witnesses for Him.

Dear Father, make me pure within. May my interests, my desires, my thoughts, and my feelings be pleasing in Thy sight. Through Jesus, amen.

Just Lucky

"And their works do follow them" (Revelation 14:13).

How much does luck have to do with success, and how much depends on hard work?

A housewife had been a loyal Detroit Tiger baseball fan for many years. Her husband was an ardent follower of another team. The year the Tigers won the pennant he claimed they were just lucky, while his team, he insisted, was just as good a team but had been "unlucky." The Tigers had all the breaks.

While luck may have its place in baseball and in other areas of life, why is it that those who are the luckiest always seem to be the ones who work the hardest?

A student wins a scholarship. Was he just lucky? Did he just happen to know the right people, and be in the right place at the right time? Abraham Lincoln said, "Prepare yourself, and someday your chance will come." And it wasn't luck that took him from a log cabin in Illinois to the White House in Washington, D. C. He prepared himself and was ready when his chance came.

Someone has said "Good luck is a lazy man's estimate of a worker's success." If a man sees another reach a goal he himself is unwilling to pay the price to reach, you may hear him say, "Oh, he's just lucky."

But is it just luck when a minister has an inspirational message; the choir sings a beautiful anthem; a teacher presents an effective Sunday-school lesson;

27

or a Christian is a leading soul winner? The verse at the beginning of the devotion says that our works will follow us. And as people see the results of our work, they can tell how much was luck and how much was work. What we sow, we will reap, and we cannot depend on luck for a good harvest.

> The heights by great men reached and kept
> Were not attained by sudden flight,
> But they, while their companions slept,
> Were toiling upward in the night.
> —*Longfellow*
> "The Ladder of St. Augustine"

Let us never be guilty of thinking that our success is due only to our own hard work. Without the Lord's help and blessing all our hard work would be to no avail. May we ever give Him the glory for whatever we are able to accomplish in this life.

Heavenly Father, we give thanks for the privilege of work and for the way in which You have blessed our efforts. In Christ's name, amen.

Standing Alone

"Be strong and of good courage, fear not . . . for the Lord thy God . . . will not fail thee, nor forsake thee" (Deuteronomy 31:6).

The class was having a lesson in civilian defense and the teacher had announced a mock air raid. "Here goes the siren," she said, making a long wailing sound that was supposed to represent an air raid siren. All the class, with the exception of one, dived under their seats. "Michael," the teacher cried, "why are you so unconcerned? Don't you know this is war and an air raid is on?"

"Yes, Miss Simpson," Michael replied, "but there ought to be at least one hero in the crowd."

It is hard to be the only one taking a stand when everyone else seems to be going in the other direction. A mother returned from watching her son in a basic-training graduation parade, and boasted to a neighbor, "Everyone was out of step except my son."

But we don't mean being out of tune with the whole world. We're speaking of having the courage to stand for something we know is right, even when everyone else takes the opposite stand. For example, when sitting with a group and hearing them spread a false rumor about someone, do we speak out? Or do we just sit there figuring that as long as we don't join in the gossip, we're not at fault?

Sometimes if we have the courage to stand for the right, we give confidence and encouragement to others. A Christian girl attended a staff Christmas party at which cocktails were served. When the waiter came to pour the drink, she very politely said no. A friend sitting next to her said, "Why didn't you take it? I'm a Christian and I drink."

A non-Christian across the table, seeing the girl refuse her drink, followed suit and later told her, "It is hard for me to turn down a drink, but seeing you refuse gave me the courage I needed."

An evangelist once suggested that when we feel discouraged and think we are alone we should:

Think of Gideon's three hundred in their places.

Think of the two who said, "We are able to take the land."

Think of the three Hebrew children in the fiery furnace.

Think of Daniel alone in the lions' den, and take courage. It is better to stand alone and be right than to follow the crowd and be wrong. Remember, when you stand for the right you are standing with God, and that makes all the difference in the world.

Dear Lord, give us courage to stand for that which is good in Your sight, even though the world may be against us. In the name of Jesus, amen.

When the Master Is Gone

"And if I go and prepare a place for you, I will come again, and receive you unto myself; that where I am, there ye may be also" (John 14:3).

Some of us have been in the position of working for an employer who had to be away from the office for two or three weeks at a time. Before he left, he gave us specific instructions. He knew what would come in while he was gone and would tell us what to do. He alerted us for any emergency and told us whom to contact. And he always made sure that we knew where we could reach him in case something arose that he alone knew how to handle.

When he returned, we went over the rush items together, then he would check up on the assignments he left to see that they were carried out. Perhaps he offered suggestions for future use, then the routine work settled down until he prepared for another trip.

Each of us is in a similar situation every day. Two thousand years ago the apostles were astonished to hear their Master say He was leaving them. For three years they had been working for Him, obeying His commands. Now He was leaving. But He was not leaving them without instructions. There was still work to do and since He would not be there, it was up to them to do it.

He wanted the whole world to hear the gospel, and instructed His followers to "Go into all the world."

He wanted the helpless to be looked after. "Pure religion . . . is this, To visit the fatherless and widows in their affliction" (James 1:27).

He wanted churches to be built and His kingdom to be enlarged. He wanted sinners converted, believers edified, and Christians to be His witnesses.

Jesus has given us specific instructions in His Word, the Bible. No other guidebook is needed. There are things that may arise that only He can handle, but He has left word that He may be reached through prayer. Too often we try to take care of the situation ourselves, then when we get in a complete mess, we turn it all over to Him. If we would get our instructions first before starting out, perhaps the work would not have to be done over.

The day is coming when He will return! He will go over the assignments He has left us. How faithful are we in carrying them out? Payday will soon be coming! Are you ready?

Dear God, we thank You that Jesus has promised to return. May we be found ready when that day comes. In the name of Your Son, amen.

The Wisdom of Age

"Bow down thine ear, and hear the words of the wise, and apply thine heart unto my knowledge" (Proverbs 22:17).

A missionary, speaking at a church, made the remark that the "church looked like a healthy church." By this he meant that he saw a good mixture of children, teen-agers, young married couples, middle-aged couples, and older people. He then made the comment that a church without older people suffers a great loss as the younger ones have no one to look up to, no one to respect, no one to encourage them as they go through their trials.

It may be that times change, and older folks seem "old-fashioned" as they look on this modern generation, but has human nature changed so much? The words of David and Solomon in the Psalms and Proverbs still correctly describe human nature today. David said, in Psalm 1:1, "Blessed is the man that walketh not in the counsel of the ungodly, nor standeth in the way of sinners, nor sitteth in the seat of the scornful." "The fool hath said in his heart, There is no God" (Psalm 14:1).

Listen to what Solomon had to say: "These six things doth the Lord hate: yea, seven are an abomination unto him: a proud look, a lying tongue, and hands that shed innocent blood, an heart that deviseth wicked imaginations, feet that be swift in running to mischief, a false witness that speaketh lies, and he that soweth discord among brethren" (Proverbs 6:16-19). Doesn't that sound like today?

"Withhold not correction from the child: for if thou beatest him with a rod, he shall not die" (Proverbs 23:13). "Favour is deceitful, and beauty is vain: but a woman that feareth the Lord, she shall be praised" (Proverbs 31:30). Times have changed, but our emotions are basically the same: love, hate, envy, vanity, and anger, to name a few.

It has been noted that, in societies such as that of the Chinese, there is far less juvenile delinquency because the youth are taught to respect their elders. In so honoring them, the young people learn a great deal. The elderly have a place in the home and in the community; they feel needed and wanted.

Certainly in the family of God we should show this same kind of respect and love for those older in years as well as those who are older in the faith. We need their wisdom; we need their sense of humor; we need their understanding. How precious are the elderly "servants of God" who are still in our midst!

Heavenly Father, how thankful we are for those who have laboured before us, who have kept the faith. Help us to learn from them that we, too, may teach others. In the name of Jesus, amen.

Taming the Tongue

"Let the words of my mouth, and the meditation of my heart, be acceptable in thy sight, O Lord, my strength, and my redeemer" (Psalm 19:14).

Sitting at the breakfast table, the husband and wife could look out the window and see the little dog next door. They not only saw him, they heard him. What a noise! This lonely little fellow had been barking since past midnight.

The couple kept close watch to see if they could discover what was causing the commotion: a squirrel, perhaps, or maybe another animal. But they could see nothing except the leaves that were blowing around the yard. Apparently, he just wanted to hear himself bark.

Is that little dog's constant barking like our conversation? Do we sometimes talk when there is really nothing to say? Do we just hear a few "leaves" of gossip perhaps that are being blown around? Or do we just like the sound of our own voice?

A woman who was known for her gossip and harmful rumors was once visited by her minister who had brought with him a pillowcase of feathers. "Take them and strew them in the street," he instructed. The woman did this. "Now pick them up," he told her.

The woman protested, "But I cannot. The wind has blown them away."

"So also you can never pick up the stories your lips have spoken," the minister concluded.

Timothy talks about women who "learn to be idle, wandering about from house to house; and not only idle, but tattlers also and busybodies, speaking things which they ought not" (1 Timothy 5:13).

Listen to what Peter says: "For he that will love life, and see good days, let him refrain his tongue from evil, and his lips that they speak no guile" (1 Peter 3:10).

And James adds, "The tongue can no man tame; it is an unruly evil, full of deadly poison" (3:8).

Our prayer should be, "Lord, help us to control our lips that the words which we speak may be only for Your glory."

Take Time to Smell the Roses

"To every thing there is a season, and a time to every purpose under the heaven" (Ecclesiastes 3:1).

It was Monday morning. A young mother sat on a lawn chair, sighing with weariness. The past week her family had all been sick with the flu. On top of that, friends with family problems had been staying in her home. The company's dog had kept her awake during the night, so in the early morning hours she arose and slipped out to the yard where all was peaceful and still.

Later her six-year-old daughter joined her and suddenly said, "Look at the roses, Mommy!" A little surprised, the mother noticed a bush in their front yard, not far from her chair. She marvelled at the beautiful, fragrant pink roses that were in bloom.

"You know," she admitted to her daughter, "there has been so much to do lately, I've been too busy to even smell the roses."

It is sad that we become so rushed with our duties —things we feel have to be done—that we do not take time to enjoy life. Does that ironing have to be done today? The windows washed? The furniture polished? Would the house fall apart if you took your children for a walk or to the park? Read them a story from the Bible? Sang around the piano for awhile?

An old lady from the country went for a train ride for the first time. She had looked forward to this trip with great pleasure and wanted so much to enjoy it. However, it took her so long to get her basket and parcels adjusted, her seat comfortably arranged, and the shades right, that she was just settling down to enjoy the trip when the conductor called out the name of her station.

"Oh, my," she said, "if I'd known that the journey was going to be so short, I wouldn't have wasted my time fussing."

We don't know how long our journey through this life will be, so let's not waste time fussing. We need to decide what is important and necessary, what can wait awhile, and what we can simply leave out of our lives. Children have a way of growing up quickly. You will not always have them with you. How many more years will your parents be there for you to call or visit? That neighbor needs to know about Jesus—now. Classes must be taught each Sunday. You may not be able to keep a "model" home but is it really that important? Don't rush through life trying to do everything at once. Take time to smell the roses.

Dear heavenly Father, how thankful we are that You have given us families to care for, homes to keep, and services to render. May we ever use our time wisely doing the things that count the most in Your kingdom. In the name of Your Son, amen.

Turning Over the Key

"In all thy ways acknowledge him, and he shall direct thy paths" (Proverbs 3:6).

The story is told of a man who dreamed that God appeared to him, asking for the keys to his life. The man gladly gave God all the keys but one small one. When the Lord asked if that were all the keys, the man admitted that he had withheld the key to a tiny closet in his heart. God told him that he must trust Him in all things.

The man tried to bargain with God but to no avail. He realized that his whole future hung in the balance. He must trust God completely in order to have God trust him to carry His Word. Finally he gave in to the Lord.

As the dream went on, God looked into that closet and began to clear it out. Then He filled it with something much better. The man suddenly realized that he had been holding on to sham jewels when God was willing to give him the real thing. God replaced the idol that had been eating out the man's life and filled his heart with His Spirit.

This reminds us of the story of the rich young ruler. He came to the right person—Jesus. He asked the right question—"What lack I yet?" He received the right answer—"Sell what thou hast, and give to the poor . . . and come and follow me." But he made the wrong decision and "went away sorrowful." He chose to hold on to his worldly riches rather than accept eternal wealth from Jesus.

What is the one thing keeping you from complete

happiness with Christ? Is there one habit that is hard to give up? Are you unwilling to forgive? Have you refused to do the job the Lord has asked you to do? Do you neglect to spend that extra time with Him in Bible reading and prayer? Have you spoken to your neighbor about accepting Christ? Do you need to replace that hatred, envy, or jealousy that is in your heart with love?

The verse at the beginning of this devotion has two parts: if we will acknowledge Him in all our ways, then He will direct our paths. Give Him the key to that one little closet today.

Gracious Father, take my life and use it as You will. Give me the strength to give up whatever might keep me from obeying You. For Jesus' sake, amen.

God's Handfuls

"My God shall supply all your need according to his riches in glory by Christ Jesus" (Philippians 4: 19).

A little boy loved peanuts. One day he went into a grocery store with his mother. The storekeeper invited him to take a handful of peanuts from a large barrel, but the boy refused. Finally the storekeeper said, "Then I'll give you some," and he dipped his hand into the barrel.

"Thank you," Willie said, accepting the peanuts that filled both his small hands.

Outside the store his mother asked, "Willie, what was the matter with you? Why didn't you take the peanuts when Mr. Phillips told you to?"

"I wanted him to hand them to me," Willie replied. "His handfuls are lots bigger than mine."

In James 4:2, 3, we are told, "Ye have not, because ye ask not. Ye ask, and receive not, because ye ask amiss." Our poor finite minds just cannot comprehend all that God wants to do for us, and we ask so little, compared to what He can give.

A minister served a church that was heavily in debt and he made it a matter of earnest prayer. A stranger, calling on the minister one day, said he had heard about the church's financial problem. He laid a blank check on the minister's desk, saying, "Fill in the amount you need and I'll be back later to sign it."

The minister thought, "He doesn't realize how much we need. I'll just put down half the amount. He probably won't even sign that."

Within an hour the man returned, gave the check a hasty glance, signed it, and hurried away. The minister looked at the check and recognized the name of a very well-known and wealthy philanthropist, one who could easily have given the entire amount the church needed. Then thinking how he had prayed for the full amount and had settled for half, the minister exlaimed, "Oh, man of little faith! I will never doubt again."

What is your problem? Is it spiritual? Financial? Physical? Mental? Is it a problem with the children? A problem concerning your husband or a relative? Whatever it is, God says, "Ask, and ye shall receive, that your joy may be full." Remember, God's handfuls are bigger than ours. Let Him do the giving.

Great God, we do thank You for Your generous gifts, Your bountiful love. Forgive us when we become forgetful. Through Jesus, amen.

Clearing Away the Dust

"This one thing I do, forgetting those things which are behind, and reaching forth unto those things which are before, I press toward the mark" (Philippians 3:13, 14).

A teacher was preparing for the first class of the morning. Going to the blackboard, she reached for a piece of chalk only to find it buried in a pile of white dust left from the day before. Slowly she cleaned the blackboard ledge of yesterday's dust and thought, with a touch of humor, of the words which were erased last night that had caused this dust.

Suddenly a very real truth came into her mind, "All of yesterday's dust should be cleaned away before I begin a new day." After a silent prayer, the teacher began her new day with eyes brighter and chin held higher. All the dust of being sorry for what might have been, of being disappointed when things did not go as planned, of being worried over trifles, of being impatient with slow results, was cleared away.

We've all seen the little sign, "Today is the first day of the rest of your life." Forget about the problems of yesterday. Start over again today. Some couples have agreed never to end a day angry with each other. There may be times when they will talk into the early hours of the morning, but they know when they go to sleep, the misunderstanding will have been cleared up, and they can look forward to the new day.

Hannah Whitall Smith in her book, *The Christian's Secret of a Happy Life*, gives us some good counsel along this line: "Never indulge at the close of an action in any self-reflective acts of any kind, whether of self-congratulation or of self-despair. Forget the things that are behind the moment they are past, leaving them with God. When the temptation comes, as it always does, to indulge in these reflections, either of one sort or the other, I turn from them at once and positively refuse to think about my work at all, leaving it with the Lord to overrule the mistakes, and to bless it as He chooses."

What a blessed promise has been given to those who obey God's Word. "If we confess our sins, he is faithful and just to forgive us our sins, and to cleanse us from all unrighteousness" (1 John 1:9). God, too, clears away the dust from our lives.

Dear God, how grateful we are that You have promised to forgive our sins. Give us strength to overcome the temptations that are ours. Through Jesus, amen.

44

Beside the Still Waters

"He leadeth me beside the still waters" (Psalm 23:2).

> Lord, I would clasp Thy hand in mine,
> Nor ever murmur nor repine.
>   Content, whatever lot I see,
>   Since 'tis my God that leadeth me.
> —*J. H. Gilmore*

How much it means to have the Lord's hand clasped in ours! It puts us on a very personal basis. When we slip, He is there to catch us and He will never let us fall.

We can be content when God leads us for we know that He would never lead us anyplace that would be damaging or wrong for a Christian. And how wonderful to know that when we are weary of the rush and bustle of our everyday duties, He will lead us beside the still waters. Doesn't this almost paint its own picture—a mountain scene, with a quiet, still stream, birds singing, and a tired traveler, kneeling beside the stream to refresh himself. There is no nervous tension here, no need for tranquilizers, no migraine headaches "since 'tis my God that leadeth me."

According to an old sheepherder, "Every shepherd knows that sheep will not drink gurgling water. There are many small springs high in the hills of the Holy Land whose waters run down the valleys only to evaporate in the desert sun. Although the sheep need the water, they will not drink from these fast-flowing streams. The shepherd must find a place where rocks or erosion have made a little pool, or else he fashions with his hands a pocket sufficient to hold at least a bucketful."

Have you been having one of those days, weeks, or months? Perhaps there has been sickness; family problems; too much month left after the money is gone; problems with the children; just not enough time to do all the things that need to be done and your soul is tired. Turn to Him and let Him lead you . . . "beside the still waters."

Kind heavenly Father, lead us the way that You want us to go. May we ever seek Your times of refreshing. Through Jesus, amen.

Accentuate the Positive

"But the fruit of the Spirit is love" (Galatians 5:22).

Christianity is positive! Christianity is active! Christianity shows itself in how we treat others.

Many religious bodies put great stress upon doing or not doing certain things. They pass laws as to how the members may dress; where they may go; how often they must come to services; what foods they must abstain from. While most of these rules may be good as far as they go, they are putting all the stress on the negative side of religion. We need rules, but we cannot get so wound up in this negative aspect that we forget the positive side.

Jesus said, "Love thy neighbour as thyself." That takes real Christianity. "Love your enemies, bless them that curse you, do good to them that hate you, and pray for them which despitefully use you, and persecute you" (Matthew 5:44). "Let your light so shine before men, that they may see your good works, and glorify your Father which is in heaven" (Matthew 5:16). This is positive thinking and acting. James puts it this way: "Pure religion and undefiled before God and the Father is this, To visit the fatherless and widows in their affliction" (1:27). Letting others know that you love them and care about them means far more than putting on a religious front or adopting a pious attitude.

Loving is giving. Loving is sacrificing. Loving is giving up something you want to make someone else happy. A marriage counselor said that true love is saying, "I love you and want to make you happy whatever it may cost me."

That is Christ's kind of love. He loved so much that He gave . . . His life!

Few people know that less than a century ago a commission was set up in Japan to consider Christianity as the state religion. The commission, however, brought in a negative report. The reason was not that they didn't agree with Christianity, but that "the moral condition of the people professing Christianity hardly recommended the faith."

We need to do more than *profess* our Christianity. We need to *possess*—possess the love of God. The love we show someone today will spread through the neighborhood, the city, the state, and into the world. Only when all men have love in their hearts, will there be peace on earth.

Heavenly Father, grant that we may have love for our families, our friends, those we don't know, and even our enemies. In the name of Him who loved us, even Jesus, amen.

The Good Old Days

"For ask now of the days that are past, which were before thee" (Deuteronomy 4:32).

So often we hear people wishing for the good old days and sometimes we wonder why. As we think of our children and the various illnesses they have had, and how they were treated by the various "mycins" and injections, we realize that in the good old days they might have been just a statistic. Science has made great strides in medicine, communications, transportation, and other fields.

Why would people want to go back to the good old days? Perhaps they miss the old-fashioned honesty, when a handshake sealed the deal. Now we need a contract in triplicate, witnessed by a notary public.

We long for a return of family life, when the home was the center of activities, when children respected their parents, and discipline was not a forbidden word. Community life meant helping and sharing with others. Then, via the party line, help for an emergency could be summoned within minutes. Now a girl is stabbed to death, while thirty-seven people watch, and do nothing. They simply don't want to get involved.

There was a lot of work in the good old days but people still seemed to find time to enjoy themselves. Nowadays, after an eight-hour day we expect to be entertained by the TV, or go out in search of something more exciting and expensive.

The good old days certainly had some advantages over today, but would we really want to go back to them if we could? Think of keeping house without our modern appliances! Imagine having to travel by horse and buggy! No wash and wear clothing, no central air conditioning, no frozen dinners! When we feel the desire coming upon us to return to those good old days, we need to count our blessings. Think of what God has given us and done for us, and then make the best of a bad situation or a depressing day.

We can never return to the days that are past. God has not promised us a long life in the future. All that we have is today. With God's help, make it the best day that you can, for yourself and for others. Learn to be thankful for each day that God gives you.

Precious Father, thank You for the time that You have given us on this earth. Help us to use this day to Your glory. In His name, amen.

Set the Temperature

"But as for you, ye thought evil against me; but God meant it unto good, to bring to pass" (Genesis 50:20).

A minister once remarked in his sermon, "If you don't like your neighborhood, change it. You have the power to change your surroundings."

Someone else has made the statement, "We may not be the sole creators of the atmosphere in which we live, but I once saw a lily growing in a swamp."

We can change the atmosphere in which we live. Perhaps we should alter that statement to read, "Let God change you, and through you He can change the surroundings." Often we try too hard in our own strength to change things, rather than allowing God to help us.

For years, a Christian lady attended church faithfully. Her husband refused to even darken the door of the church. He was a well-liked fellow, but had no interest in spiritual things. Then the church began a prayer and fasting program on Saturday nights and this man's name was put on the prayer list. Soon he began dropping bad habits one by one because, as he said, he couldn't afford them anymore, but others realized that God was speaking to him.

Then one Sunday morning, during a series of special meetings, the husband made his decision for Christ. Since that time he has not missed a single service—Sunday morning, Sunday evening, revival, prayer meeting, or otherwise. He was in his 70's when his life was turned over to God. His wife had remained patient all those years. She maintained a Christian atmosphere in the home, set a good example by her faithful church attendance, and reared a Christian daughter who loved and respected her dad. Had the woman let down her Christian standards her husband would never have been brought to the Lord.

We as Christian homemakers should not be like a thermometer, that only records the temperature and does nothing about it, but rather like a thermostat that sets the temperature. We can set the spiritual temperature of our home if we first let Christ change us and live through us. Our surroundings can be changed!

Dear Father, help us to realize the importance of our faithfulness. Give us the strength to maintain a Christian environment. Through Jesus, amen.

Recipe for Happiness

"And we know that all things work together for good to them that love God, to them who are the called according to his purpose" (Romans 8:28).

You would not eat a cup of flour or sugar by itself, nor would you drink a cup of salad oil. None of us likes the taste of baking powder or vanilla. Yet we take these ingredients, mix them up, and end up with a great variety of cakes, cookies, and other desserts for our families to enjoy.

That particular problem you're going through now—perhaps a husband or boy in service, financial difficulties, or illness in the home—right now it doesn't look as though it could ever work out to anything good. But God takes this experience, mixes it with one in the past, and one to come, and then we can see the reason for it all.

A Christian girl, walking home from work one night, lost a ten-dollar bill. She was very upset because it was the money she had saved for her mother's Christmas present. The next morning as she got ready for work, her employer called, asking if she could come into work at eight, instead of ten.

Grumbling a little, she hurried to make the 7:30 bus, only to see it pull out ahead of her.

Walking the eighteen blocks to work, her head down in discouragement, she saw a ten-dollar bill lying in a puddle. If she had gone in to work at ten, someone else would have found the bill. If she had caught her bus, she never would have seen the money. Thinking back over the events that had just transpired, the girl realized that all things had worked together for her good.

Too often, we hear the first part of the verse quoted, omitting the part that mentions that this good happens to those who love God and are doing His will. We cannot expect God to continue to bless us if we refuse to follow Him. Only when we surrender to His will can we look for His promises to be ours.

Dear Father, help us to remember that with each promise and blessing, there is a responsibility for us to carry out. Through Christ, amen.

I Am Only One

"I can do all things through Christ which strength-eneth me" (Philippians 4:13).

A minister once said, "I never hear a symphony orchestra without thinking of the importance of the individual and the necessity for cooperation. No man can make a symphony orchestra. The combined talents of many musicians, working in harmony and unity, are needed to achieve the desired results. No one is more important than anyone else because each player is essential to a perfect whole."

It is so easy to say, "I am only one. What can I do?" Many people use this reasoning for not going to the polls. "What difference could my vote make?" Elections have been lost by one vote. Andrew Johnson was saved from impeachment by one vote. Bills on the legislative floor have been passed or defeated by one vote. As Edward Everett Hale said,

I am only one, but still I am one.
I cannot do everything, but still I can do something;
And because I cannot do everything
I will not refuse to do the something that I can do.

A great crowd of spectators jammed the Los Angeles Coliseum in June of 1945 to watch a mighty pageant honoring the city's war heroes. After a mock battle scene had driven home the seeming helplessness of the individual, silence fell, and only the voice of the emcee could be heard: "Perhaps you sometimes say to yourself, my job isn't important because it's such a little job. But you are wrong.

The most obscure person can be very important. Let me show you what I mean."

The giant searchlights bathing every corner of the great Coliseum were shut off, transforming the day-like splendor of the arena into total darkness. Then the speaker struck a match and in the blackness the tiny flame could be seen by everyone. "Now you can see the importance of one little light," the emcee said. "Suppose we all strike a light." In an instant, matches were struck all over the stadium until nearly 100,000 pinpoints of light illuminated the summer night. The audience gasped with surprise. Quickly and effectively they understood the power of the individual life.

God is concerned about the individual. "Whosoever believeth in him"; "Whosoever will, let him take the water of life freely." God also expects each one to work for Him—"Go *ye* into all the world." You can't win the entire world to Christ single-handedly, but then you don't have to. There are countless others with the same commission. Just do your best. With God's help it will be enough.

Dear Lord, may we ever be mindful of the importance of the individual, no matter how insignificant he may seem. In the name of Jesus, amen.

Angels in Dirty Clothes

"Look not on his countenance, or on the height of his stature; because I have refused him: for the Lord seeth not as man seeth; for man looketh on the outward appearance, but the Lord looketh on the heart" (1 Samuel 16:7).

It may be that we think better of a person than what his inward character would warrant, but usually it's the other way around. We see only the outward appearance and do not see the latent potential in a person. We need to have the ability to see what is inside that person and help him make it a reality. We have to be able to believe that he can be more than what he appears to be on the outside.

This is especially true with children. We have to look not at what they are now, but to what they can become with God's help. The little girl with a torn dress and straggly hair, the boy who is always tipping his chair and pulling pigtails—inside these youngsters there is someone longing to be loved, someone saying, "Here I am, please notice me."

Look beyond what you can see to what God can see. He looked beyond Zacchaeus in the sycamore tree to Zacchaeus a repentant sinner. He looked beyond Matthew the tax collector to Matthew the apostle. Jesus looked beyond Peter who denied Him to Peter who preached His gospel on the Day of Pentecost. And He looked beyond Saul of Tarsus, the persecutor of Christians, to Paul, the preacher, the writer, and world evangelist.

The story is told of a sculptor who spent his days chipping away at a huge block of marble. He was watched daily by a small boy who sat quietly, never disturbing him with comments or questions, his eyes reflecting growing curiosity and wonder. Finally, as the figure of a sleeping lion emerged as the result of the artist's deft strokes, the boy's curiosity and amazement exploded in the question, "But how did you know that lion was in there?"

How do we know what lies within our children or those we teach? Oil producers take crude physical resources and refine them. In the same way, God gives us as parents and teachers the raw materials and we, through prayer and with His help, must refine them and help them to develop in their Christian lives.

Dear God, help us to realize the importance of developing the potential in those around us. May our lives be used to the fullest in Your service. In Jesus' name, amen.

My Brother's Keeper

"And the Lord said unto Cain, Where is Abel thy brother? And he said, I know not: Am I my brother's keeper?" (Genesis 4:9).

This question has echoed down through the centuries: "Am I my brother's keeper?" For some, it will never be answered because they do not want to know the truth!

This is such a personal question. It does not ask, "Should my neighbor help my brother?" or even, "Should the welfare help my brother?" but rather, "What can *I* do?"

Who is my brother? Christ explained it so simply in the story of the good Samaritan. My brother is anyone who needs my help.

Why are people unwilling to be their brother's keeper? To help, you must first love, and to love, you must become involved.

Hannah Whitall Smith in *The Christian's Secret of a Happy Life,* says, "We never care about the little details of people's lives unless we love them. It is a matter of indifference to us as to what the majority of people we meet do, or how they spend their time. But as soon as we begin to love anyone, we begin at once to care."

If we become involved, we have to admit we care. A television personality once said in an interview, "If you do not want to become involved, then don't get married. Never have children. Forget about your family. Anytime you love someone, you become involved."

But the wonderful thing about becoming involved with others is the reward it brings—seeing a husband and wife reunited; a child get well; a former mental patient face society; an alcoholic leading a normal life. All these, and many other joys you can share when you become your brother's keeper.

"He's not heavy, he's my brother."
  Well-known words of poem and song.
"He's not heavy, 'cause I love him"
  And he carried him along.

Are we still our brother's keeper?
  Yes, his burdens we must bear.
And we'll find he isn't heavy—
  If we love and really care.

Dear God, help us to be truly concerned about others just as You are concerned about us. In Jesus' name, amen.

A Desert Place

"Come ye yourselves apart into a desert place, and rest a while" (Mark 6:31).

We all need a "desert place" where we can "rest a while." From the moment we arise, the day is full of activity. Breakfast must be prepared, lunches fixed, husband sent off to work, and children to school. Then begin the routine tasks of picking up, making beds, washing dishes, mopping, dusting, a break for lunch, and begin all over again.

A lady once gave a reading in Sunday school in which she spoke of "making beds that wouldn't stay made, washing dishes that wouldn't stay washed, and spanking children who wouldn't stay spanked." Isn't that the way it often seems? If you have preschoolers at home, you do not have the break of seeing all the children off to school. Instead, you try to clean around little pairs of active hands and feet. Then you turn around and wonder how they could possibly have spilled that bowl of cereal or glass of milk in so short a time.

We all need a time just for ourselves. It may be to nap, to write some letters, or to read the book that's been borrowed for so long.

In the Biblical story of Mary and Martha, it bothered Martha that she had all the work to do in the kitchen while Mary went out and sat at Jesus' feet. When Martha complained, Christ reminded her that "Mary hath chosen that good part, which shall not be taken away from her." She had found her desert place.

Our desert place may be a quiet bedroom, a park bench, perhaps a visit to a shut-in—some place where we can regain our equilibrium and realize "there's always tomorrow." Not everything really has to be done today. The ironing will still be there, the dishes can wait a half hour longer. Take time today to re-discover God—in nature, in literature, in yourself.

> Come ye apart and rest awhile,
> Enjoy the blessing of His smile.
> Come ye into a desert place
> And look upon the Saviour's face.
>
> Just rest, or read, or kneel and pray,
> And there gain strength for each new day.
> To find contentment in your heart,
> Out of the world—come ye apart!

Dear Father in heaven, may we ever look to You for the rest and peace we cannot find in the world. In Jesus' name, amen.

Use It for God

"But he that had received one went and digged in the earth, and hid his lord's money" (Matthew 25:18).

How many people have you heard say, "But I don't have any talents." In the Matthew account of the talents (which was actually money, in this case) we notice that even after the person with the two talents doubled them, he still didn't have as many as the man with the ten talents. Some of us will never be as talented as others, but we should be thankful for the talents we do have and strive to develop them for God's glory.

A seminary wife and her husband were getting ready to take their first church. She was especially talented. She could write, play various musical instruments, enjoyed singing, did chalk drawings, and was very good at working with children. Another girl told her, "Oh, if I could only do as much as you can."

Upon hearing this, the first girl replied, "I would gladly trade them all if I had your knack for housekeeping and decorating, and your talent for cooking and sewing. And you're such a good listener! Those are all very important qualities for a minister's wife."

Someone has said, "There is no limit to what can be accomplished in this world as long as no one cares who gets the credit." Not everyone can be up in front. God's work is made up of big jobs and little jobs. If we are too big to do the little jobs that need to be done, then we will be too small to do the big jobs that come along.

You may never be able to teach a class, sing a solo, or play the organ, but don't sell yourself short. The church nursery needs workers to lovingly care for the babies. Sheets must be laundered each week. You say you can bake a cake or fry chicken? Meals taken to the sick, shut-ins, or bereaved are a real blessing. If you can drive a car, you have a very important talent that can be used in the Lord's work. A smile to someone who is discouraged can be more effective than a beautifully-rendered solo. Take inventory of the abilities that God has given you. Then find where you can best use them in His service. You will be blessed and God's work will benefit.

Dear Father in heaven, help me to find the talents that have been given me and use them to Your glory. In the name of Jesus, amen.

Hold My Hand

"Hold thou me up, and I shall be safe" (Psalm 119:117).

A little girl, shortly after moving to a new home and being unused to stairs, fell down the entire flight. After the fall, whenever she wanted to come downstairs she would call out to her father or mother, "Hold my hand."

Millions of people are searching for security today. Some will take a job with less pay because it is steady. Many girls are marrying not for love, but for security. Through the problems of life it is good to have Someone to whom we can say, "Hold my hand" and know we will be safe. But if we hold His hand, we must walk in the way that He leads.

Picture a small child walking with his parents. Everything is fine until they come to a corner and the parents say, "Turn this way."

"No," the little boy may protest, "I want to go this way." Very seldom will the parent change his destination to suit that of the child's so it means the child must bend his will to that of someone who knows best.

Often in our Christian lives, things may go fine until we come to a corner. "Come this way," Christ may say, but we protest, "I want to go this way." Just as the child cannot continue to hold his parent's hand if he goes another way, so when we decide to go our own way, we cannot say to God, "Hold my hand." Holding to God's hand comes only with obeying His commands. And then we find real security.

There's never any need of falling,
    Just hold to the Saviour's hand.
Can you not hear His sweet voice calling?
    Just hold to the Saviour's hand.

Whene'er you feel your faith is drifting,
    Just hold to the Saviour's hand.
He will be there, your spirit lifting.
    Just hold to the Saviour's hand.

When life is o'er, and death is nearing,
    Just hold to the Saviour's hand.
Still trust in Him, nothing fearing,
    Just hold to the Saviour's hand.

His arm is strong and yet so tender.
    He says, "My child, you're safe from harm."
Be not afraid and trust Him ever.
    Just hold to the Saviour's hand.

Dear heavenly Father, may we ever keep our hand in Yours and go where You want us to go. In the name of Jesus, amen.

So Short a Time

"Remember how short my time is" (Psalm 89: 47).

So many things happen to remind us how fast time goes by—the wedding of someone we knew when "he was in diapers"; an invitation to a class reunion; and, of course, those birthdays that roll around with regularity (and children to remind us which birthday it is).

Time certainly gets away from us, but where does it go? A minister's wife once said, "It's hard to get people to give time to the church anymore. First comes their new homes, then their new cars, then the country club and golf course, and if there is any time left over, it goes to the church."

This should give us food for thought. As Christians, we need to be good stewards of our time as well as our income. If we were to give the Lord just a tenth of our time it would mean two hours and twenty-four minutes each day for spiritual things. Do we give even a fraction of that in prayer and Bible reading, not to mention service to others in His name?

Someone has said, "We major in minors and minor in majors." That is, we spend too much time on things that are not important, while neglecting the things that will last for eternity.

How much time do we spend with our children? Do we take time to look at a sparrow in the yard, or listen to something that happened in school, or are we too busy? Do we dare let the ironing go while we read to the little ones. Even chores that have to be done can be made a family project. Learning to work together is an important lesson in Christian living.

Let us make sure we have our priorities straight. Time is short. Make the most of it.

Eternal God, give us the ability to discern what is important so that we do not waste the precious gift of time. Through Christ, amen.

A House Divided

"And if a house be divided against itself, that house cannot stand" (Mark 3:25).

In almost every community throughout the nation we see signs of construction. With the population explosion, there is need for more houses, more apartment buildings, more "senior citizen" complexes.

In all this growth, what is happening to the homes? One writer stated that "four walls do not make a home," and a once-popular song observes, "A house is not a home." A house alone is cold and empty. It needs a family with love and concern to make it a home.

In all of this growth, what is happening to the family unit? Obviously, in many homes the family is no longer united. Everyone is busy with his own work, friends, recreation, and interests. There is hardly time to sit down and enjoy a family meal, let alone spend an evening sharing a common project, or attend a church service together.

When is the last time you sat together, as a family, during the worship service? Are you taking time to instill in your little ones a knowledge of God and

His Word? Do you really listen when your teen-ager feels like talking? Do you and your husband actually communicate with each other? With the rest of the family? Grandmother, are you simply "turning off" the younger generation because they wear their hair too long or dress in such extreme fashions? They may be seeking your attention and advice. Sunday-school teacher, that restless, noisy youngster may be absorbing more than you realize. Have the patience and faith to try to reach him for the Lord.

God put great emphasis on the home and family life. It is up to Christ's followers to try and restore the home and family to their rightful place. Our nation can be no better than its homes. If our homes are not united, how can our nation stand?

Many the problems in this complex world,
Furious the questions that daily are hurled,
But there is one that so often comes—
How can we best build strong Christian homes?

What are the materials needed today
To keep our children from going astray?
How can we teach them the lessons of life,
When they're surrounded by turmoil and strife?

First, a reverence for God's Word,
Faith and willingness to follow the Lord.
And the obedience to His command:
"Honor thy parents and live long in the land."

Great God, help us to realize the importance of teaching and working with our children. May we set the example for them by being faithful to You in our day-by-day living. In the name of Jesus, amen.

No Occupation

"Her children arise up, and call her blessed" (Proverbs 31:28).

How much can you remember about your early childhood days? One mother remarked, "I never realized, as I grew up, that our house was often messed up and there were holes in the plaster until I looked through some photographs one day. Then I realized we had been poor. All I can remember is my mother welcoming our friends each night; taking time to put together jigsaw puzzles; singing around the piano with us; sewing doll clothes; and making hot chocolate and popcorn for us. I never wondered till later years when she had time to do her housework."

Mothers are strange creatures. They say "I'm not hungry," when food is scarce, or "I'd rather have the crust," if there are just two pieces of bread left in the wrapper. They wear last year's dress because the children need new shoes. They get up early to prepare Sunday dinner while the rest of the family sleeps, then smile when the others wonder why Mother isn't ready for church as soon as they are.

Today's women are led to believe that they cannot possibly fulfill themselves unless they seek a career outside the home. Their education, their talents, their very lives will be wasted if they remain simply wives and mothers. Is this really so? Since when has home-making and child-rearing ceased to utilize every available talent and training a woman can have?

A working knowledge of economics, psychology, dietetics, medicine, child-guidance, interior decorating, and labor-management—not to mention home economics—are needed and used by the successful wife and mother. On top of this she needs great physical stamina, patience, a sense of humor, self-control, an unselfish disposition, impartial judgment, and a heart of love. It is a twenty-four hour job, with no real vacation, but the compensations more than make up for this.

What more fulfilling job could there be than that of a mother? What a great thrill it is to see her sons and daughters grow up to become good citizens and servants of God. How happy she is to know that her home is tidy and attractive, and her husband happy and satisfied. She may never make it on the census taker's list—he doesn't consider homemaking and child-rearing as occupations. So what? The duties may be many, but then the rewards are great.

Dear Father, how thankful we are for women who are willing to use their lives ministering to their families. Help them to see the importance of their work. In the name of Christ, amen.

Pray Without Ceasing

"Evening, and morning, and at noon, will I pray, and cry aloud: and he shall hear my voice" (Psalm 55:17).

Is prayer important? Does it really do any good to pray? Are things changed by prayer, or is it just a coincidence? Would it have happened anyway, even if someone hadn't prayed?

It's strange, but even people who do not profess to being "religious" will admit to having prayed during some crisis in their lives. Perhaps the difference between these persons and the Christian is, that the first uses prayer as a rope to pull only in time of trouble. The Christian keeps up his prayer life on a daily basis and when trouble comes, he has only to remind the Lord that he belongs to Him, and that God has promised to look after His own.

God answers prayer in strange ways. A motto reads, "Prayer changes people and people change things."

In a house with three small children, with money scarce and the cupboards bare, the mother prayed. The children were somewhat skeptical. What good would prayer do? Shortly after, a lady came to the door with some money she owed the mother, but had forgotten about. When she remembered it, she decided to bring it over the next day, but something

73

persisted, "No, take it tonight." And she came before the grocery stores closed. Just a coincidence? You couldn't convince three hungry children of that.

We must add feet to our prayers. We often pray that God will bless the sick and be near to them. But have we visited, or written, or tried in some way to cheer the sick? The story is told of a man who was praying for a friend of his who was in need. He prayed, "Lord lay Thy hand on him." And the Lord replied, "You are my hand."

And another thought: it would be foolish for an orchestra to tune up after the concert is over—they tune up before. So, as Christians, we should "tune up" our hearts through prayer before we go out to meet each new day.

Abraham Lincoln once said he was often driven to his knees in prayer by the realization that there was nowhere else to go. We can stay on our feet facing the world only after we have stayed on our knees facing God.

Dear Father, we thank You for the privilege of prayer and for the answers You give us. In Your Son's name, amen.

The Twenty-Third Psalm

From the Kiowa Indian language

(Translated by Isobel Crawford)

"The Great Father above a Shepherd Chief is the same as, and I am His, and with Him I want not. He throws out to me a rope. The name of the rope is Love. He draws me, and draws me, to where the grass is green and the water not dangerous, and I eat and drink and lie down satisfied. Some days this soul of mine is very weak, and falls down, but He raises it up again and draws me into trails that are good. His name is Wonderful.

"Sometime, it may be in a little time, it may be a little longer, and it may be a long, long, long time, I do not know, He will draw me into a place between mountains. It is dark there but I will not pull back, and I will be afraid not, for it is in there between those mountains that the Great Shepherd Chief will meet me and the hunger I have felt in my heart all through this life will be satisfied. Sometimes this rope that is Love He makes into a whip and He whips me, and whips me, and whips me, but afterward He gives me a staff to lean on.

"He spreads a table before me and puts on it different kinds of food, buffalo meat, Chinamen's food, white men's food, and we all sit down and eat that which satisfies us. He puts His hand on my head and all the tired is gone.

"He fills my cup till it runs over. Now what I have been telling you is true. I talk two ways not. These roads that are always good will stay with me all through this life, and afterward I will move to the big Teepee and sit down with the Shepherd Chief forever."

Is the meaning so much different? "The Lord is my shepherd; I shall not want. He maketh me to lie down in green pastures: he leadeth me beside the still waters. He restoreth my soul: he leadeth me in the paths of righteousness for his name's sake. Yea, though I walk through the valley of the shadow of death, I will fear no evil: for thou art with me; thy rod and thy staff they comfort me. Thou preparest a table before me in the presence of mine enemies: thou anointest my head with oil; my cup runneth over. Surely goodness and mercy shall follow me all the days of my life: and I will dwell in the house of the Lord for ever."

The important thing is, do you know the Shepherd? Are you allowing Him to lead you? Do you believe that He will guide you, protect you, and prepare a place for you? He cannot lead unless you are willing to follow—obediently, unhesitatingly, and unquestioningly.

O God, our shepherd, may we ever be ready and willing to follow where You lead. In Jesus' name, amen.

God's Fluoroscope

"Do ye look on things after the outward appearance?" (2 Corinthians 10:7).

We have all probably had the experience of meeting someone for the first time and thinking, "I surely wouldn't want to know him. Why, the way he looks . . ." We need to remind ourselves that beauty is truly "skin deep." Physical attractiveness, or the lack of it, can be misleading.

Five-year-old Missy struggled into the house holding a yellow kitten she had found. In spite of the fact that it was skinny, filthy, and of doubtful background, Missy was madly in love with the kitten. For the next several weeks girl and kitten were inseparable until one day the little creature wandered away and couldn't be found. Missy was inconsolable.

In an effort to comfort the sad little girl, her grandmother went downtown and bought a Persian kitten that cost a large sum of money. It was a beautiful creature, but with no apparent warmth or affection in its nature. When Missy was presented with the kitten, she appeared entirely unappreciative.

Missy's mother scolded the little girl for her attitude. "Missy," she said, "you are acting very naughty about this. You lost your kitten, so Grandma bought you this beautiful Persian kitten, but you're not satisfied with it."

Missy tried to swallow the lump in her throat and replied, "But Mamma, you don't understand. This kitten is pretty on the outside, but it's the inside of the kitten that counts."

A college girl who disliked all insects began dating a science major. Part of his work involved collecting various insects and studying their everyday habits. As the relationship between the two young people deepened, and the naturalist began to teach the girl more about the insects he was studying, she also began to be interested in them. One day she exclaimed, "Insects were once so ugly to me, but since I learned to love Jim, he has taught me how beautiful these tiny creatures can be."

Some people may not appear to have physical beauty. But, if we could use God's fluoroscope to see what is inside their hearts, we would see just how beautiful they are. We would no longer notice the physical imperfections, but love them just as God does. Remember, it's the inside that counts.

Father in heaven, help us to look beyond a man's physical appearance to his inner beauty and character. May we ever strive to be pure within. Through Jesus, amen.

Fair-Weather Christians

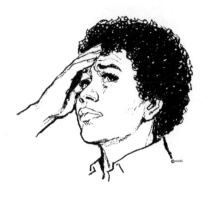

"Time would fail me to tell of [those] . . . who through faith . . . stopped the mouths of lions, quenched the violence of fire, escaped the edge of the sword . . . had trial of cruel mockings and scourgings, yea, moreover of bonds and imprisonment: . . . were stoned, they were sawn asunder, were tempted, were slain with the sword . . . afflicted, tormented" (Hebrews 11:32-37).

A cartoon shows a man getting his car and repair bill from a garageman who tells him, "I think it'll be okay now if you avoid hills, sudden accelerations, traffic jams, heavy loads, sharp turns, and long trips."

Have you ever met a person like that car? He is all right as long as everything goes his way. If there are no battles to fight, no days of sickness, no lay-offs at the plant, no family problems, and the world is rosy, his song is bright.

What happens to that person when someone

spreads a rumor about him; a new family comes into the church and the man of the house is immediately voted onto the church board ahead of him; a person with less seniority at work is given the promotion he had been expecting; illness strikes; bills pile up. What happens to his song then?

In the book, *The Greatest Faith Ever Known,* Fulton Oursler describes in detail how the early Christians were tortured and murdered at the hands of Nero. In spite of this, the early church continued to grow. Persecution didn't stop Christianity, it only made it more attractive.

Perhaps the real drama about this book is not in the content itself, but in the fact that while halfway through its writing, Mr. Oursler died of a heart attack. His daughter, April, rather than blaming and questioning God for taking her father, studied the manuscript and finished the book in the same dedicated style her father had used.

Here is the secret to real Christianity. When the reverses come, when there are problems—finances are scarce; sickness comes; maybe a friend has betrayed us; we must not look back, but ahead. Anyone can be good when there are no temptations or problems. It takes real dedication to carry us through the periods of stress, heartache, and disaster. The fact that we are alive shows that God still has work for us to do. Let us never question God's reasons for sending what He does, but rather use these difficulties to prove our faith.

Heavenly Father, give us strength and courage that we may be pleasing to You even in the most trying times. In our Saviour's name, amen.

Opening Up the Roses

"For ye have need of patience, that, after ye have done the will of God, ye might receive the promise" (Hebrews 10:36).

A mother began looking for her five-year-old boy after not seeing him around for awhile. "Johnny, where are you?" she called. She looked all over the house, then she looked out the window and saw him walking in the garden. "What are you doing?" she asked, as he came in the door.

"Helping God," he replied.

"Helping God?"

"Yes, I was opening up the roses for Him."

We all know that roses open in their own time and all we do cannot make them open sooner. But what about rushing ahead of God's time to make things come to pass? Someone has said, "God never hurries, but He's always there on time." Most of our headaches and heartaches in life are caused by impatience—trying to solve matters in our own way and in our own time. We go around opening roses, thinking that we're helping God.

"But," you might say, "I get so discouraged." There is nothing wrong with discouragement if it doesn't happen too often nor last too long. The sun has a sinking spell every night, but it rises again the next morning. The secret is in rising one more time than we fall.

We need patience to believe that our trials will not last forever. Dr. W. T. Purkiser in his book, *When You Get to the End of Yourself*, says "God does not offer us a way *out* of the testings of life. He offers us a way *through*, and that makes all the difference." One elderly man said that his favorite Bible phrase was, "And it came to pass." Time will change many of the problems we now face. We need to cultivate the patience to wait for that time.

What would we think of a farmer who planted a field of corn and waited until about the first of August, then went out and plowed up that field in disgust because the corn was not ready to pick? God takes time to work out His purposes. He may allow you to become discouraged, heartsick, and disappointed, but don't rush to find the solution. Let God have His time and way. He will open the roses when the time is right.

Dear Father, grant us the patience and faith to wait upon Your will. Forgive us when we question, or rush ahead to seek our own solution. Through Jesus, amen.

Burdens Into Bridges

"Most gladly therefore will I rather glory in my infirmities, that the power of Christ may rest upon me" (2 Corinthians 12:9).

A biologist tells how he watched an ant carrying a piece of straw that seemed almost too heavy for it to drag. The ant came to a crack in the ground that was too big to cross. It stood still for a time, as though perplexed by the situation, then put the straw across the crack and walked over on the straw.

How do we react to our problems? We talk about them to our friends; we complain about them; but have we ever thought of converting our burdens into bridges? Then they would bear us up instead of us bearing them up.

During the depression a man lost his job, his money, his home, and his wife, but he held to his faith—the only thing he had left. One day he stopped to watch some men doing stonework on a huge church. One of them was chiseling a triangular piece of stone. "What are you going to do with that?" asked the man.

The workman replied, "See that little opening way up there near the spire? I'm shaping this stone down here so it will fit in up there."

Tears filled the man's eyes as he walked away, for it seemed that God had spoken through the workman to explain the trials through which he had been passing. "I'm shaping you down here so you'll fit in up there."

When things are going well, when life is easy and

83

we have no burdens, we get too self-confident. We begin to think that we are completely self-sufficient. Then God sends us a problem or a burden to bear. How helpless we suddenly become. Our burdens keep us close to God. Perhaps God does not allow everyone to bear a burden—only those who are willing to put their trust in Him. Just as an old grandfather's clock cannot run without the heavy weight that has to be pulled to the top regularly, so a Christian cannot grow without burdens. When the burdens come, God uses them to "get us in shape down here" so that someday we'll "fit in up there." Don't let your burdens get the best of you—use them as bridges.

Dear Father, thank You for sending problems so that we might be tested and strengthened. Help us to put our trust in You, rather than relying on our own strength. In Your Son's name, amen.

Preparing the Way

"And he shall prepare the way before me" (Malachi 3:1).

A man was telling a friend about his job in a banana packing plant and how tiring it was. "I have to separate all the good bananas from the bad ones," he explained.

"That doesn't sound too hard," the friend remarked.

"But it is," the man insisted. "Decisions, decisions all day long!"

Life is not easy. Teen-agers have exams facing them in school; housewives, a big day ahead with housework, errands to run, PTA meeting at night; breadwinners go out into the hustle and bustle of the business world, working for a promotion, trying to make ends meet. All these problems seem so impossible when we try to do them on our own.

We don't have to walk alone, though. We have Someone who has promised to go before us, to prepare the way, to help us with these decisions.

A young couple was working at an Indian mission in Arizona. The husband had become well acquainted with one of the teen-age Indian boys. When it was discovered that the boy had not eaten in three days, the man asked his wife to invite the boy for dinner. She hesitated, because she had already invited guests for dinner—a couple who had just recently moved from another state. She had hoped through this invitation to witness to the couple and interest them in the work of the church.

Her husband noticed her hesitation and assured her that they could invite the Indian boy another day. After praying about it, she decided that it was the right thing to do, and she asked the boy to dinner. Imagine her surprise when she discovered that the new man was part Indian. Everyone had a wonderful day of fellowship. That night, as she thought about the events of the day, the woman was reminded that when the Lord speaks, He also prepares the way.

Has there been something the Lord has asked you to do, but you have put it off, worrying that it wouldn't turn out right? "He shall prepare the way before me." We need never be afraid when we walk with Him.

Dear God, thank You for ever preparing the way for us. Thank you especially for sending Jesus to show us the way to heaven. In His name, amen.

In Love With God

"I love them that love me; and those that seek me early shall find me" (Proverbs 8:17).

Sometimes we see a couple who have been married for many years and they anticipate each other's every word and move. One asks, "Did you . . ." and the other replies, "Yes, I did." How do they do this? They have been so close to each other for so many years that they are constantly in touch. They have taken time throughout those years to learn, understand, and try to please each other.

A brother and sister who had sung together for many years in revivals and special services often would go from one song to another without previous practice. Somehow they sensed the other's thoughts. They were on the same "wave length," so to speak. And even though they are now separated by two thousand miles, they still keep in touch, because of their love for each other.

If we are truly "in love with God," we will be constantly in touch with Him. When we are rushed and tension begins to rise, a whispered prayer can ease our troubled minds. When we receive good news, or a loved one is made well, a quick "thank You" is breathed to Him. The title of a song states, "Just a Whisper from the Lord." We need to be living so close to Him that we can hear His slightest whisper.

It would be strange if a fellow told a girl he loved her but never went to see her or called her on the telephone. She would soon doubt his love.

And aren't we guilty of the same thing? When we became Christians, we promised to put the Lord first in our lives. Then instead of reading the Bible, we read the newspapers and TV Guide. A television program or sporting event takes the place of our church attendance. We buy new clothes, a better car, and redecorate the living room. There's nothing left for the Lord. If we really are "in love with God," we will put Him and His will first in our lives.

Father, forgive us for putting the world ahead of You. Help us to show our love and gratitude by giving you first place in our hearts. In the name of Your Son, amen.

The 101st Blow

"I have planted, Apollos watered; but God gave the increase" (1 Corinthians 3:6).

The great nineteenth-century British statesman, Benjamin Disraeli, was asked how he bravely went on without seeing the results from many of his efforts. He answered, "Have you ever watched a stonecutter at work? He will hammer away at a rock for perhaps one hundred times without a crack showing in it. Then at the one hundred and first blow it will split in two. It was not that blow alone which accomplished the result," smiled Disraeli, "but the one hundred others that went before it as well."

Paul, in the above Scripture verse, has come to the realization that in all of his missionary travels he has planted much seed, but other preachers and missionaries who followed him watered the seed he had planted. There were probably many cases where he did not see the results of his labors.

Whether you are a Sunday-school teacher, a missionary, or a housewife trying to witness to a good friend, you may not see the results of the seed you have planted. But at the same time, you may see a person converted through a seed that was planted many years before by a Christian friend or Sunday-school teacher.

Also, while you may not see that particular person helped, some of the seed may drop on other ground and a bystander may receive help from your labors.

A Christian schoolteacher had a charge in a small community in South Dakota. The one church building in the town was unoccupied so she obtained permission to use it for a Sunday school, later conducting regular worship services. Living six miles out in the country was a rancher, with seven children, who did not attend the services, so the schoolteacher began sending him a postcard each week.

This went on for fifty-two weeks. The next week the rancher said to his wife, "We're going to church next Sunday. If we don't, that schoolmarm is going to run herself poor sending us them postcards." So the next Sunday they headed for Sunday school and stayed for church. At the next revival service they were all converted, and a son later became a missionary.

The fifty-second postcard—the one hundred and first blow—whatever is necessary, don't give up.

Father, we thank You for the seed that was planted by those who refused to give up. Help us to have that same kind of determination to continue in our service. Through Christ, amen.

Thanks for the Memory

"Enter into his gates with thanksgiving, and into his courts with praise" (Psalm 100:4).

Someone has suggested that we establish a thankful memory bank. Whenever something good happens to us, we should write it down on a slip of paper and put it in our thankful memory bank. Then on one of those days when nothing seems to go right, we can draw a slip out of our bank and remember how God has blessed us in times past.

But in order to do this, we must learn how to develop a thankful memory. It is so easy to remember all the uncomplimentary remarks people say about us, but how about the good things they say? Are they so hard to remember? Then we need to write them down, not to give us a big head, but to encourage us on those days when our faults seem so prevalent.

Perhaps we bought an inexpensive appliance from a local department store and the appliance refused to operate properly. Before we call the store with angry words we will later regret, we should think back to the ninety-nine times we bought things from that same store that are still usable.

Maybe a telephone operator seemed rude or not as helpful as she could have been. How many times have we needed the services of an operator and she was unusually helpful even though we may not have had all the information required?

Was the choir a little off key on a particular Sunday morning? The preacher's sermon a little too long? The Sunday-school teacher not well prepared? Someone didn't speak to you at church? What about the mornings the choir's song blessed your heart, the sermon challenged you, the Sunday-school lesson inspired you, and people went out of their way to greet you and perhaps said they had missed you when you were absent?

We sometimes criticize our news media for dwelling on the bad news. But how about us, aren't we guilty of this very same thing? Dwell on the happy, the pleasant, the good. Give thanks to God for these things rather than complain about the problems and hurt feelings we encounter from day to day. Let us develop a thankful memory bank.

Thank You, God, for allowing so much good to come to us. Help us ever to be grateful for your blessings. Forgive us when we complain. In Your Son's name, amen.

Destination Heaven

"For how long shall thy journey be?" (Nehemiah 2:6).

Have you ever been homesick and then felt the excitement as arrangements were made for a trip home? What hurry and scurry to get things packed! Finally the day arrived and you were on your way.

You probably stopped on your trip to eat, then on second thought, decided to take some with you to have on hand.

The roads in some places looked unfamiliar and you wondered if you were lost. But then you realized that the driver had been this way before and he knew where he was going. Detours were man-made but you soon found yourself on the highway again.

You sometimes wondered if you would make it, there were so many delays. But suddenly—there you were, and there were loved ones waiting to meet you. They helped you down the last step and encircled you in their arms. "Welcome home," they said.

We as Christians are also taking a journey to the place God has prepared. Often our souls get hungry for more of God, so we go to church, to the Bible, to our knees; eat of the Bread of Life and drink at the Fount of Living Water until we are full. Then we decide to take some along with us and that bit of Scripture in the hour of temptation or the verse of song on that gloomy day is sufficient to meet our needs.

The path sometimes looks strange but Christ tells us He has walked this way before and He knows every fork and bend in the road even before we come to it. There are times when we think we know a short cut, an easier road, so we detour. But after a few miles, we must turn back to God's highway.

We do not know when we will reach our destination. There is so much work to be done, we often stop to find someone to accompany us on our journey. But someday we will reach the end and there will be Someone to meet us. He'll reach out His nail-scarred hand to help us across the Jordan River, and then will say, "Welcome Home."

Our fare has already been paid on Calvary. Let us start traveling today.

Eternal God, thank You for allowing Your Son, Jesus, to pay the price for our salvation. May we ever look forward to that day when we shall be at home with You. In Jesus' name, amen.

You Are Important

"But even the very hairs of your head are all numbered. Fear not therefore: ye are of more value than many sparrows" (Luke 12:7).

I'd like to close this book with a personal illustration. I don't think I ever realized the importance of one small punctuation mark until I began typing this manuscript and the question mark broke on my typewriter. Do you realize how often you use a question mark when you are writing? We just take it for granted, but after the manuscript was typed and I had to go through page by page and ink in all the question marks, I knew I would never take that punctuation mark for granted again.

There is probably no career or occupation in which a person is taken more for granted than that of a housewife or mother. As long as the dishes are clean; the clothes are washed, ironed, and hanging in the closet; things are put away where everyone can find them; the rest of the family seldom realize the work that goes behind it all. It does get discouraging, occasionally, and we find ourselves wondering, "Do I really count as an individual or am I just a servant? Am *I* important?

They say, "You never miss the water till the well runs dry." A mother is usually more appreciated if she has to be gone for some reason, on a trip or to the hospital, and the father is left in charge. After he has put the girl's dresses on backwards a few times, refereed the children's fights, and cooked a few meals, he begins to realize the value of his mate, and the children their mother.

You are only one, but you are important . . . to your family, to your friends, and, most of all, to God. Remember, one life can change the whole world.

Perhaps you don't have a family to take you for granted. You live alone—no one needs you or really cares about you. You feel very much alone and un-loved at times. But remember, God cares about you. Jesus gave His life for you. You are needed in the kingdom of God. There is a place you can serve where no one else can. Let God use you and show you the way. You are important!

Eternal God, thank You for loving and caring for each of us. Lead us and strengthen us to do the work You have for us. May we ever realize the importance of each soul You have created. In the name of our Redeemer, amen.